All About Word Problems

Written by Joyce Markovics

rourkeeducationalmedia.com

Scan for Related Titles
and Teacher Resources

www.rourkeeducationalmedia.com

PHOTO CREDITS: Cover: © Tony Campbell, Anna Utekhina; Page 1: © Courtneyk; Page 3: © CEFutcher; Page 4: © DjordjeZ, Page 5: © Nataliap; Page 6, 7: © GlobalP; Page 6, 7, 8, 9, 18, 19, 20, 21: © DNY59; Page 10, 11, 12: © Andrew-Howe; Page 13: © doglikehorse; Page 18: © EEI-Tony; Page 19: © Andrewkyzmin; Page 22: © Mari, Tiler84; Page 23: © Treb999

Edited by Jill Sherman

Cover design by Tara Raymo

Interior design by Jen Thomas

Library of Congress PCN Data

All About Word Problems / Joyce Markovics
(Little World Math)
ISBN 978-1-62169-890-6 (hard cover)
ISBN 978-1-62169-785-5 (soft cover)
ISBN 978-1-62169-989-7 (e-Book)
Library of Congress Control Number: 2013936807

Also Available as:

Rourke Educational Media
Printed in the United States of America,
North Mankato, Minnesota

Rourke
Educational Media

rourkeeducationalmedia.com

customerservice@rourkeeducationalmedia.com • PO Box 643328 Vero Beach, Florida 32964

Word problems are little math puzzles that we read to solve.

To solve a word problem, read it carefully. Then turn the words into numbers.

Finally, write out the math problem
and find your answer!

Let's practice adding!
The black pony ate one apple.

Three birds are looking for lunch.

Then two birds fly away.

3 − 2 = 1

How many balloons are there in all?
Add the three numbers together. There
are 8 balloons in all!

$$4+3+1=8$$

Sometimes, we have to add and subtract to solve a word problem. Do you want to try?

There are nine kittens in one basket.
There are two kittens in another basket.

How many kittens are there in all?

$$9 + 2 = ?$$

Add the kittens. 11 kittens!

What happens when two kittens jump out of the baskets? How many kittens are left?

Subtract two kittens from eleven kittens.

$$11 - 2 = ?$$

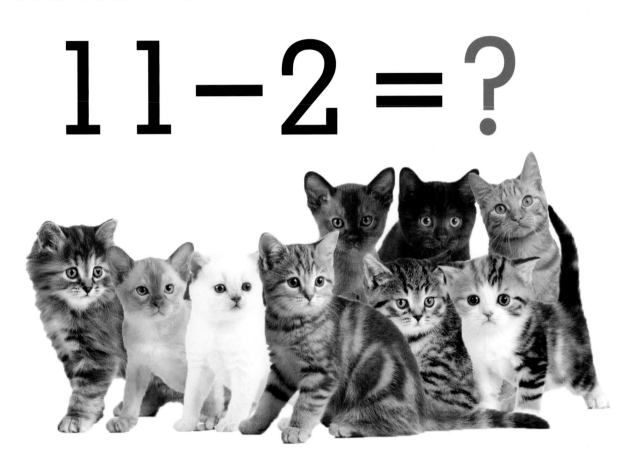

The answer is 9 kittens!

Can you solve a word problem all by yourself? Give it a try.

A boy has $5. He buys two cupcakes. Each cupcake is $2.

$2 each

Then subtract that amount from $5.
How much money does he have left?

Did you have fun figuring out the answer?

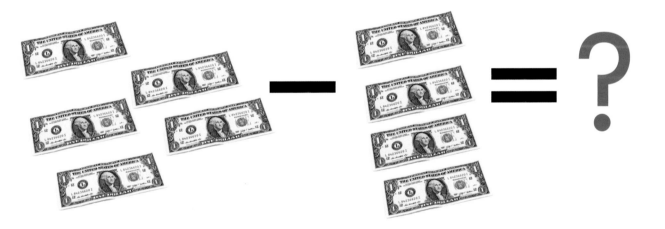

$$5 - 4 = 1$$

Index

Websites

www.gscdn.org/library/cms/84/10184.pdf

www.k-5mathteachingresources.com/support-files/1st-gd-addition-problems.pdf

www.k-5mathteachingresources.com/support-files/1st-gd-subtraction-problems.pdf

About the Author

Joyce Markovics is a writer and editor. She shares her home in New York City with her husband, Adam, and a menagerie of pets that includes a spirited house rabbit named Pearl and a crooning frog. She has written over 20 books and enjoys thinking and writing about abstract concepts for young readers.

Meet The Author!
www.meetREMauthors.com